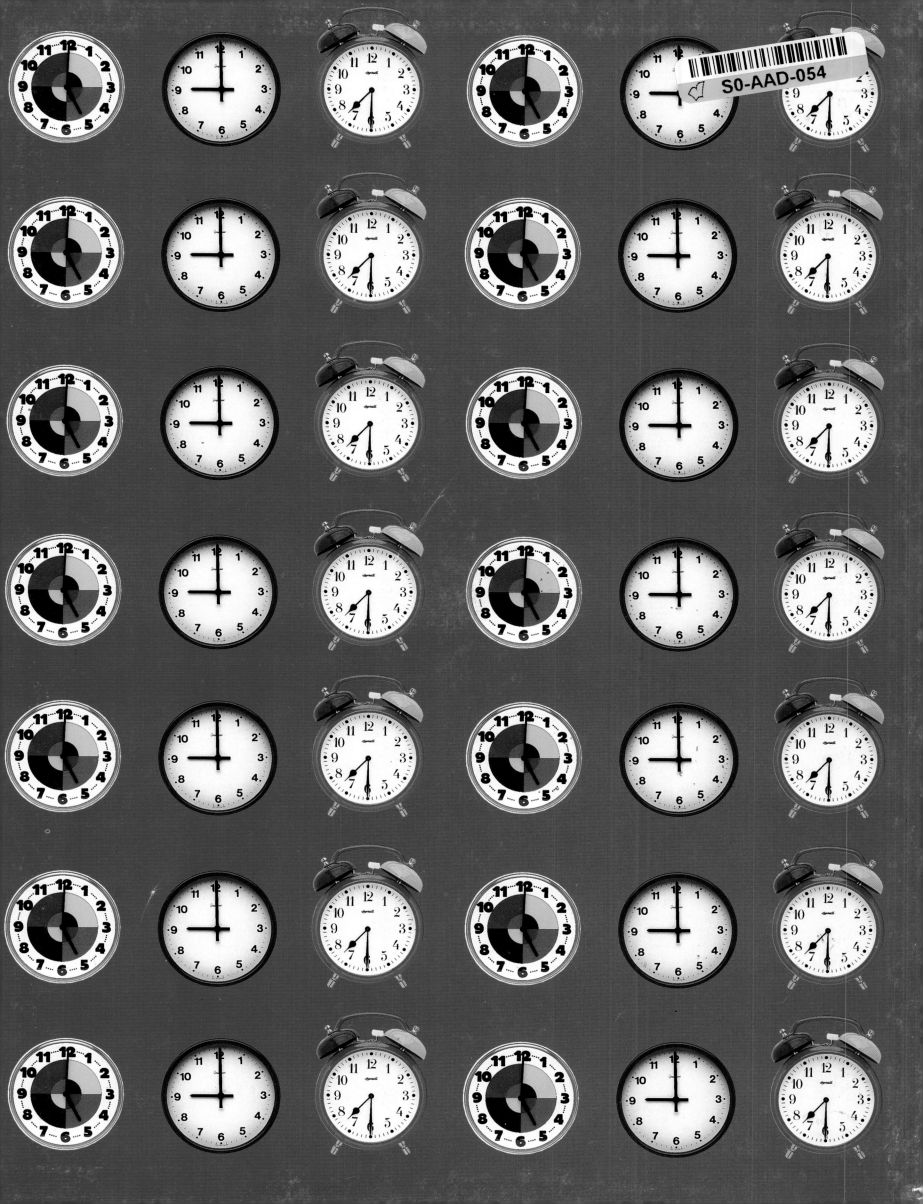

MY FIRST
BOOK OF
TIME

Claire Llewellyn

DORLING KINDERSLEY EDUCATION
London • New York • Stuttgart

A DORLING KINDERSLEY BOOK

Editor Sheila Hanly
Art Editors Nicki Simmonds, Jane Coney
U.S. Editor B. Alison Weir
Senior Art Editor Rowena Alsey
Production Marguerite Fenn
Managing Editor Jane Yorke

Mathematics consultants Elizabeth Meng, Marcia K. Miller

This is a Dorling Kindersley Education edition, 1993

Library of Congress Cataloging-in-Publication Data
Llewellyn, Claire
My first book of time/Claire Llewellyn. – 1st American ed.
   p.   cm.
Summary: Explains how to tell time and discusses such aspects of
time as day and night, days of the week, and months of the year.
Includes a fold-out clockface for practice.
Includes index.
ISBN 1-879431-78-5 (trade edition)
ISBN 0-7516-0501-8 (school edition)
1. Time – Juvenile literature. 2. Clocks and watches – Juvenile
literature. 3. Toy and movable books – Specimens. [1.Time.
2. Clocks and watches. 3.Toy and movable books.] I.Title
QB209.5.L54 1992   91-58194
529'.7 – dc20   CIP
                                                         AC

Color reproduction by Colourscan
Printed in Singapore by Tien Wah Press (PTE.) Ltd

Photography by Paul Bricknell
Illustrations by Julie Carpenter

Recommended for children aged four years and up.

Contents

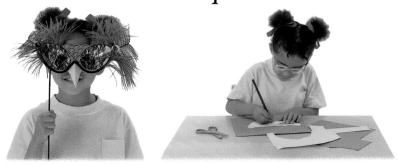

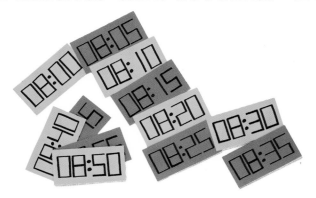

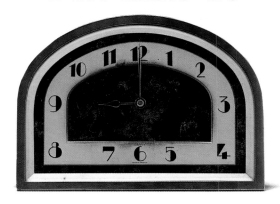

Note to parents and teachers

This is a book about time: that illusive something that seems to slip through our fingers so readily. While some of us seem to develop an uncanny ability to judge time, most of us struggle along with the aid of a timepiece strapped to our wrist or placed in strategic spots in our environment. This book addresses both of these aspects of time: the passage of time, and reading time.

A sense of time

Time is a difficult concept for children to understand. They cannot see or feel time. The same period can seem to pass quickly or slowly depending on what activity they are engaged in. Children usually begin to develop an early sense of time through becoming familiar with the patterns and sequences of events in their daily, weekly, and seasonal routines. They also learn to read cues that indicate the passage of time, such as the length of shadows. The sense of time grows gradually through the primary school years and often is not well developed until around nine years of age, although this can vary with the individual. As you share this book, you will be helping your child develop a sense of time.

Telling the time

Children want to learn to tell the time. It gives them a feeling of competence and independence. The ability to read a clock, however, requires certain prerequisite skills that we, as adults, may not be conscious of – until we try to help youngsters. They need to know the number symbols and their sequence. In addition, there is a need for a clearly defined sense of direction (direction of hand movement); an understanding of fractions (e.g. half past six); and a sense of equivalency (e.g. 6:50 is also 10 to 7).

Fun time

The fold-out clock will make practice fun and can be used to relate time to your child's daily routines. The experience of gaining confidence in this necessary skill will be an enjoyable one for both you and your child. The beautiful illustrations, activities, and thought-provoking questions all make this a book you can return to again and again.

Professor Elizabeth Meng
Teachers College,
Columbia University

About this book

This book has some special features to help you learn all about time.

Using your fold-out clock
Inside the back cover of the book, you will find a fold-out clock. You can use it to practice telling the time. It folds out next to any page you are reading.

Your clock has two movable hands. The short hand is red. It tells you the hour. The long hand is blue. It tells you the minute. These colors match the hands and numbers of the teaching clocks on the time-telling pages.

Remember, you can also practice on your fold-out clock without your book.

Watch the clock!
Look for this picture on the pages of this book. It tells you when your fold-out clock can help you solve a puzzle.

Words about time
As you work through the book, you will notice that some words have been highlighted in **heavier print**. These words are explained in **Words about time** on page 32.

Day and night

A new **day** begins each **morning** with the sunrise. We are active during the **daytime** – moving, working, playing, and eating. What do you do during the day?

It begins to get dark each **evening** at sunset. After a long day of work or play, we need to rest. Most people go to sleep at **night**. Can you think of any people who are awake all night?

Spot the difference

Look at the two pictures below. How can you tell which picture shows day and which night? What differences between day and night do you see?

All in a day

Birthdays are wonderful days.
But they take a whole year to come
around and then they seem to be over
in a flash! What time of day is your
favorite part of a birthday?

Morning

Is morning the best part,
when you get ready
for your party?

Afternoon

Do you enjoy the
afternoon most,
when all your
friends come
to play?

Evening

Is the evening of your
birthday your favorite
part? By then, everyone
has gone home and you
can look back over the
whole happy day!

Days of the week

Days pass quickly. Together, seven days make up a **week**. Do you know what each day is called? This **diary** shows all the special things Rebecca did in one week. What things do *you* do every week?

Monday

We went on a nature walk during school **today.** Tom and I found some pretty leaves.

Tuesday

We used our leaves from **yesterday** to make a picture.

Wednesday

I love Wednesdays! Today I went to my swimming lesson.

Thursday

After school I went to play group. We made ginger cookies. Yummy!

Friday

In music class today, I kept playing at the wrong time. I'll have to practice for next week.

Saturday

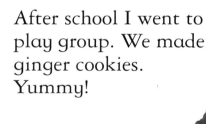

It's the **weekend.** I went shopping with Mom and Dad to buy things for a picnic **tomorrow.**

Sunday

We were out the whole day. We had a great picnic! Tomorrow is Monday. I wonder if something exciting will happen?

The months of a year

Each **month** has about four weeks. There are 12 months in a **year**. Can you name all of the months? Do you have a favorite month? In which month were you born?

Number of days in a month

Month	Days	Month	Days
January	31	July	31
February	28/29	August	31
March	31	September	30
April	30	October	31
May	31	November	30
June	30	December	31

A calendar month

Have you ever seen a **calendar**? Calendars show all the days of a month on one page. We write on a calendar to remind ourselves of the important things we plan to do in a month. Why not try to make your own calendar?

Making your calendar

1 Gather together the supplies you will need. Draw lines on the paper, as shown in the picture.

2 Write the name of the month at the top of the paper.

3 Fill in the days of the week. Check how many days there are in your month. Then, fill in the numbers for the days. Remember, months don't always begin on Sunday.

Picture dates

You can mark special **dates** on your calendar by drawing pictures instead of writing.

 Birthday   **Dentist**

Vacation   **A day out**

Haircut   **Sports**

Here are a few picture examples for you to use. You can make your own, too.

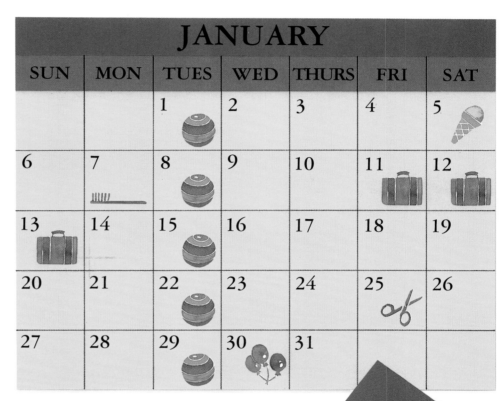

JANUARY

SUN	MON	TUES	WED	THURS	FRI	SAT
		1	2	3	4	5
6	7	8	9	10	11	12
13	14	15	16	17	18	19
20	21	22	23	24	25	26
27	28	29	30	31		

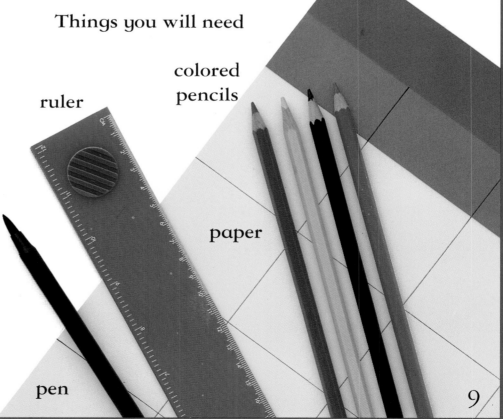

Things you will need

colored pencils

ruler

paper

pen

9

The four seasons

Spring, summer, fall, winter – these are the four **seasons** that make up our year. Each season brings a number of changes: the weather is different, the daylight is different, the length of shadows is different. These changes are very important. All living things notice them, and they begin to change, too.

The changing seasons

- What is your favorite season?
- What happens to most trees and plants in spring?
- How do animals prepare for winter?
- When do most farmers harvest their crops?
- How do you like to keep cool on a hot summer day?
- What season comes after winter?
- In what season is your birthday?

Spring

Spring days have more hours of daylight than the cold days of winter. Many animals have babies now.

Summer

In summer, daylight lasts the longest. The weather is usually sunny and hot. It's the perfect time for outdoor activities.

Why do the seasons change?

The top half of the Earth is warm and bright because it's tilted toward the sun. It's summer here.

Earth

The bottom half of the Earth is colder, because it's tilted away from the sun. It's winter here.

sun

Although we can't feel it, the Earth is always turning. It takes 24 hours to make one full turn. This is why there are 24 hours in a day. In this picture of the Earth and sun, one side of the Earth is facing the sun. It's daytime there. The other side is dark and shaded. It's nighttime there.

As it turns, the Earth also circles the sun. It takes a year to go around the sun once. The top of the Earth is tilted toward the sun and it's summer. As the Earth moves around the sun, the bottom half tilts toward the sun and the seasons change.

Fall

In fall, there are fewer hours of daylight. The leaves on most trees change color and fall to the ground. Have you ever noticed what squirrels do in the fall?

Winter

Winter days have the fewest hours of daylight. The weather becomes much colder. The nights can be frosty. In some places, snow falls.

Time to grow

All living things grow, and as they grow, they change. Observing these changes in the things around us is one way of noticing that time has passed.

Not everything takes the same amount of time to grow. Some things grow and change very quickly, while others take much longer.

See how you've grown
Find a recent photograph of yourself and one of yourself as a baby. Do you look very different now from when you were a baby? What changes do you see?

Days to grow

sprouting bean seeds

after one day

after six days

Keep the jar's lid screwed on while the seeds grow.

Try this experiment to see how quickly bean sprouts grow. Soak a handful of sprouting bean seeds overnight in a jar of water. Drain them well and leave the jar in a warm place. Rinse the seeds daily with clean water. After two days, they should start to sprout. In about six days, the bean sprouts will have grown roots and leaves.

Weeks to grow

Ducklings grow at a slower pace than bean sprouts. The tiny one-day-old duckling is covered in fluffy down. After two weeks its feathers start to grow. At eight weeks, the duck is fully grown.

one day old

two weeks old

eight weeks old

Years to grow

People grow so slowly that we usually measure their growth in years, not in weeks or days. A year is a long time. It's the amount of time between one birthday and the next. Look at these pictures of a woman at different ages throughout her life.

- How has this woman changed over the years?
- What other living things take years to grow?
- How old are you?
- How many years do you think it will take for you to become a grown-up?

1 year old	4 years old	14 years old	27 years old	58 years old

Birthday puzzle

Each candle on a birthday cake stands for one year of someone's life. Count the candles on these birthday cakes.

How old are these children? Who has the most candles?

Rebecca   Billy   Tom   Jane

- Who is the oldest child here?
- Who is the youngest child?
- Is Tom or Billy older than Rebecca?

- Can you guess how old Tom will be on his next birthday?
- Is Billy older or younger than you?

13

A world of clocks

We use **clocks** and **watches** to tell the time. Once you begin to notice them, you will see clocks everywhere. Can you imagine what it would be like if we had no clocks to help us keep track of time? All the clocks on these pages have special jobs. Can you think of any other useful clocks?

Airport clock
If you don't check the time on the airport clock, you might miss your plane.

Nurse's watch
Nurses wear these watches pinned to their uniforms. Why do you think the face hangs upside down?

Video clock
Why do we need a clock on a video recorder?

Digital clock
What do you think makes this digital clock work?

Picture clock
Brightly colored clocks are made specially for young children. Have you ever seen one like this?

Wind-up clock
You can see the insides of this carriage clock. It has a glass door at the back so you can watch the moving parts. It also has a special key that winds it up to make it work.

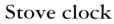

Digital watch
Can you see what makes this digital watch work?

Stove clock
A clock on a stove has a buzzer that reminds us when it's time to take food out of the oven.

Station clock
A clock at a railroad station tells people when it's time to board their trains.

Cuckoo clock
Every hour a bird pops out of a door at the top of this clock and says, "Cuckoo!"

Floral clock
This clock's numbers are made of plants! Where might you see a clock like this?

Alarm clock
How does an alarm clock wake you in the morning?

Clocks on buildings
There are beautiful and interesting old clocks on buildings all over the world. Is there a special clock on a building in the town where you live?

Clock without numbers
Sometimes it's hard to tell the time on modern clocks. This one has no numbers on it!

Grandfather clock
This grandfather clock is very tall. It makes a loud "tick-tock" noise. What sort of noise does it make every hour?

Children's watch
This watch was designed to help children learn how to tell the time. The numbers are easy to read.

On the hour

Analog clocks have two hands to tell you the time. The two hands move slowly around the **clockface**. The **short hand** tells you the **hour**. It takes 12 hours for the short hand to go all the way around the clockface. The **long hand** tells you the **minutes**. It takes 60 minutes to go around the clock.

eleven o'clock

twelve o'clock

one o'clock

two o'clock

When the long hand is pointing straight up at the 12, it tells you that it's *something* o'clock.

The short hand is pointing to the 8.

Together, the hands tell you that the time is **eight o'clock**.

ten o'clock

three o'clock

nine o'clock

four o'clock

The hands on a clock always move in the same direction, called **clockwise**.

eight o'clock

seven o'clock

six o'clock

five o'clock

These clocks show every hour of the day.
• Which clock hand moves faster?

• What were you doing at these times today?
• What is your favorite hour of the day?

16

Digital time

A **digital clock** doesn't have a face and it doesn't have any hands. It uses numbers to tell us the time.

The number before the dots is just like the short hand on an analog clock. The number after the dots is like the long hand on an analog clock.

- Are there any digital clocks in your house?
- Where else can you find digital clocks?

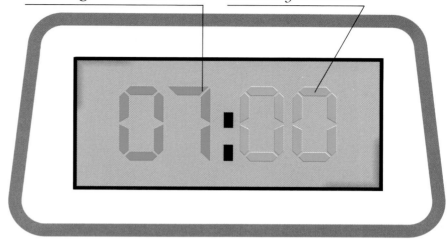

This number tells you which hour it is. It's showing the number 7.

This number tells you the minutes. It's showing 00, which means it's *something* o'clock.

Together, the numbers tell you that the time is **seven o'clock**.

Matching time

- What times do these clocks and watches show?
- Can you find the clocks that show the same time?
- Move the hands on your fold-out clock to match all the times shown on this page.

Halves and quarters

Have you ever heard people say, "It's quarter after six," or "It's a quarter to three"? Do you know what they mean? The long hand on a clock tells us about the halves and quarters. It takes one hour for the long hand to go all the way around the clockface.

After or past and to

When the long hand is between the 12 and the 6, we say the time is after or past the hour. When the long hand is between the 6 and the 12, we say it's to the hour.

Quarter after

When the long hand is on the 3, it's gone a quarter of the way around the clockface. We say it's **a quarter after**. The short hand is just past the 8, so the time is a quarter after eight.

Half past

When the long hand is on the 6, it has gone halfway around the clockface. We say it's **half past**. The short hand is halfway between the 8 and 9, so the time is **half past eight**.

18

Quarter to

When the long hand is on the 9, it has gone three quarters of the way around the clockface. It has one more quarter to go. We say it's **a quarter to**. What time does this clock show?

Tell the time

Practice telling the time on these clocks and watches.

 Can you show these times on your fold-out clock?

Start to finish

Half an hour and a quarter of an hour are useful terms when we talk about time. Look at the clocks and figure out how long Anna takes to make her mask.

start

finish

1 First, Anna traces the shape of the mask and cuts it out. How long does she take?

2 Next, Anna draws patterns on the mask. She takes another quarter of an hour to do this.

start

finish

3 Last of all, Anna sticks the pieces together. Her mask is finished. How long, in total, has it taken Anna to make her mask?

start

finish

19

Minutes and seconds

A **minute** is a much shorter period of time than an hour. It takes 60 minutes to make up one hour. The minutes are marked on the clocks below. There are five minutes between each number on a clockface. The clocks below show the time in five-minute steps around the clockface.

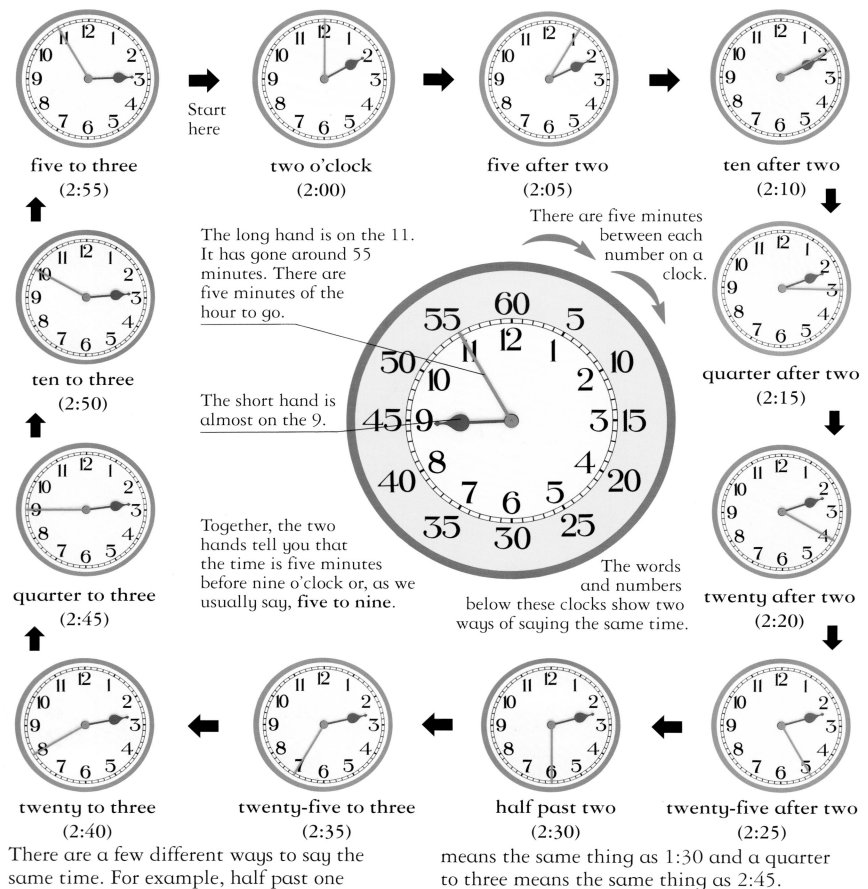

five to three
(2:55)

Start here

two o'clock
(2:00)

five after two
(2:05)

ten after two
(2:10)

There are five minutes between each number on a clock.

The long hand is on the 11. It has gone around 55 minutes. There are five minutes of the hour to go.

The short hand is almost on the 9.

ten to three
(2:50)

quarter after two
(2:15)

quarter to three
(2:45)

Together, the two hands tell you that the time is five minutes before nine o'clock or, as we usually say, **five to nine**.

The words and numbers below these clocks show two ways of saying the same time.

twenty after two
(2:20)

twenty to three
(2:40)

twenty-five to three
(2:35)

half past two
(2:30)

twenty-five after two
(2:25)

There are a few different ways to say the same time. For example, half past one means the same thing as 1:30 and a quarter to three means the same thing as 2:45.

Seconds

Seconds are very short. There are 60 of them in one minute. You can't do much in a second – maybe just sneeze or clap your hands. Some clocks and watches count out the seconds with an extra hand that moves very quickly around the clockface. Do you have any clocks with second hands in your home?

• Why do we need seconds?
• When are seconds useful for measuring time?

second hand

Just a second
See if you can beat a drum or clap your hands 10 times in 10 seconds. Watch a clock with a second hand. Were you too fast, too slow, or just right?

Find the pairs

For each of the times written below, there is a matching time on a clock or watch.

When you find a pair, cover those 2 boxes with pennies or small pieces of paper.

	1:20		Ten to eleven	
Twenty-five to ten		Five to four		2:40
	9:10		Five after seven	
Twenty-five after three		Twenty to eight		5:50

Digital clocks

Some people think it's easier to tell the time on digital clocks. This is because we can read the time exactly as it appears.

The numbers before the dots go from 1 to 12. The numbers after the dots go from 1 to 60. Do you know why?

Halves and quarters

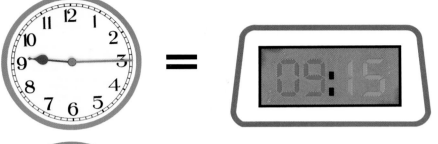

Quarter after
This digital clock shows us that it's 9:15, or a quarter after nine. On the analog clock, the long hand has gone around 15 minutes.

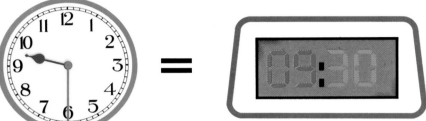

Half past
This digital clock shows us that it's 9:30, or half past nine. On the analog clock, the long hand has gone around 30 minutes.

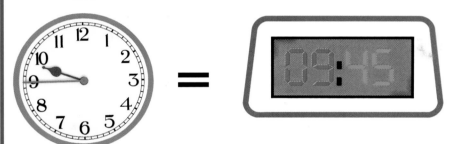

Quarter to
This digital clock shows us that it's 9:45. On the analog clock, the long hand has gone around 45 minutes. What is another way of saying what time it is?

Sixty minutes

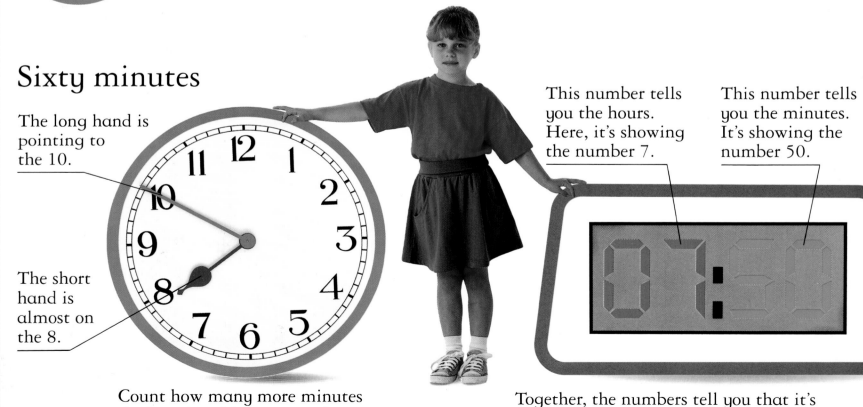

The long hand is pointing to the 10.

The short hand is almost on the 8.

This number tells you the hours. Here, it's showing the number 7.

This number tells you the minutes. It's showing the number 50.

Count how many more minutes the long hand has to travel before it gets back to the 12.

Together, the numbers tell you that it's 50 minutes after seven o'clock, or 7:50. We can also say it's ten to eight.

Tell the digital time

- What time do these clocks and watches show?
- 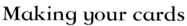 Can you move the hands of your fold-out clock to match these times?
- How many different ways can you say each time?

Clock cards

Here is a game to practice telling the time on a digital clock. You can make this game yourself, or ask an adult to help.

The game can be played by two or four players. It will help you and your friends practice counting by fives.

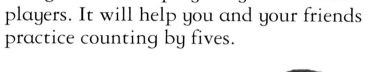

Making your cards

1 Make 24 playing cards out of stiff cardboard. (Be very careful when using sharp scissors.)

How to play

- Deal all the cards, so that each player has the same number.
- The first player puts a card face up on the table. The next player tries to lay a card alongside, with a time five minutes earlier or later than the card before.
- Players who can't find a card with the right time on it miss their turn.
- The winner is the first player with no cards left.

2 Write a digital time on each card. Start at any time, but make sure that each card shows a time five minutes after the card before.

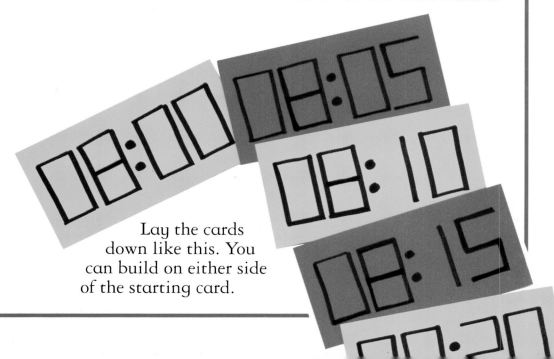

Lay the cards down like this. You can build on either side of the starting card.

The 24-hour clock

Although there are 24 hours in a day, traditional clocks are numbered 1 to 12. In one day, the short hand travels around the clockface twice.

Some digital clocks are different – they number the hours 1 to 24. This way of telling the time is called the 24-hour clock.

The time is eight o'clock. But is it eight o'clock in the morning or the evening? An ordinary clock doesn't say. But this special clock also shows the hours up to 24.

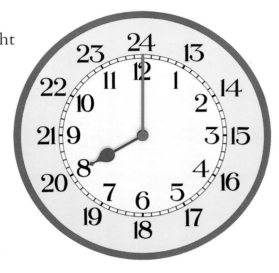

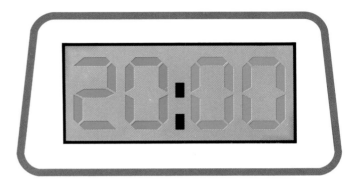

The time is twenty o'clock, which also means eight o'clock. A digital clock clearly tells us that it is eight o'clock in the evening.

Time line

On a 24-hour clock, you start counting the hours from **midnight**. Up until **noon**, the hours are numbered 1 to 12. After noon, they are numbered 13 to 24.

midnight   noon   midnight

a.m.   p.m.

24:00 01:00 02:00 03:00 04:00 05:00 06:00 07:00 08:00 09:00 10:00 11:00 12:00 13:00 14:00 15:00 16:00 17:00 18:00 19:00 20:00 21:00 22:00 23:00 24:00

Morning or afternoon?
You don't have to use the 24-hour clock to show whether a time is in the morning or the afternoon. You can use letters instead. We use **a.m.** to show that it's before noon, and **p.m.** to show that it's after noon.

After noon

When you're using a 24-hour clock, the times greater than 12 are after noon, or p.m. You convert the time, let's say 14:20, to the 12-hour clock to figure out that 14:20 is also called 2:20 p.m.

• Can you read these times and show them on your fold-out clock?

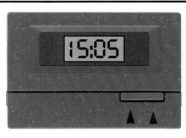

24

Time around the world

The Earth is always turning. So, as the day begins and the sun rises on one side of the world, the same day ends and the sun sets on the opposite side of the world. Isn't it amazing to think that when you're beginning your day, children in Australia are getting ready for bed?

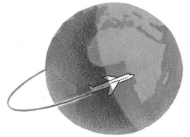

Time zones

Because of these big differences in time, the world has been divided up into 24 different time zones, one for each hour of the clock. Can you count the zones on this map?

Flying across time zones

Planes can take off in one time zone and land in a different one. Passengers have to change their watches to the new time.

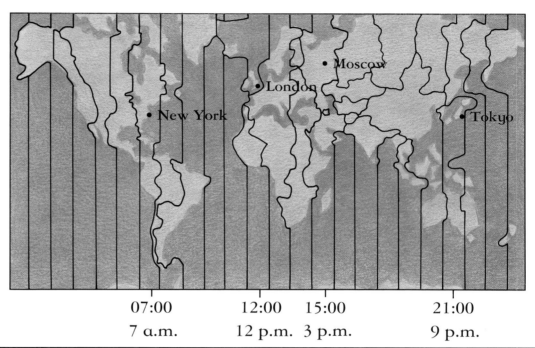

07:00	12:00	15:00		21:00
7 a.m.	12 p.m.	3 p.m.		9 p.m.

A single moment

Children do lots of the same activities all over the world. But at exactly the same moment, they may be doing very different things. What would you be doing at the same times as these children from different places in the world?

7 a.m.
07:00

New York, USA
In New York, it's seven o'clock in the morning. Bobby is getting dressed. He's got a busy day ahead of him.

London, Great Britain
In London, it's noon. Rebecca is hungry. What's for lunch today?

12 p.m.
12:00

Moscow, Russia
In Moscow, it's three o'clock in the afternoon. Mikhail is drawing a picture.

3 p.m.
15:00

9 p.m.
21:00

Tokyo, Japan
In Tokyo, it's nine o'clock at night. Yoshimi is fast asleep.

25

Measuring time

Sometimes we use clocks to measure the time we take to do things – in a race or a game, perhaps. But you don't always have to use a clock.

There are other ways you can time yourself – with a sand-timer, for example. Why not make one and try timing things for yourself?

The smaller the hole in your cone, the slower the sand will pour.

Use both hands when you pour sand into the cone.

Make a sand-timer

1 Draw a rectangle about 15 inches by 7 inches on a piece of heavy paper. Cut it out. (You should be careful when using sharp scissors.)

2 Roll the paper into a cone, leaving a very small hole at the bottom. Tape your cone together securely.

3 Put the cone in a large jar. Now pour some dry sand into the cone. Always use exactly the same amount of sand to time yourself.

Time without numbers

You can use your sand-timer to see how quickly or slowly you do certain things. Count how many times you can write your name, or hop on one foot, before all the sand runs through the timer. Race against a friend or try to beat the timer.

Balancing trick
Balance a ball on your feet for as long as you can. Can you keep it balanced for as long as it takes for the sand to run through the timer?

Speedy skipping
How many times can you skip rope before the sand runs out? Guess before you race the timer. Were you close?

*Candy race
Try picking up candies from a bowl by sucking through a straw. How many candies can you move onto a plate before all the sand runs through?

*Be sure that you use candy that won't fit through the straw.

26

Counting in seconds

Have you ever seen **timers** like these? Most of them use seconds, minutes, and hours to measure time.

Cooking timer

You can set this timer so that a bell rings when your food is cooked.

Egg timer

When is this timer especially useful?

Stopwatch

Stopwatches have a special button for timing activities. Press the button to start timing, then press it again at the finish!

Digital stopwatch

Digital watches have the same kind of timing button as analog stopwatches. Push this button and the watch counts the time in seconds.

In a fraction of a second

Stopwatches and digital watches are good for timing races. They count the time in seconds. Have you ever seen a timer for races on television? Sometimes there is less than one second between two competitors at the finish!

Ready, set, go!

Why not use a stopwatch to time a race between you and your friends? Don't just run – try hopping, skipping, and jumping. Running may take the least time, but what takes longest? Try the races again to see if you can do them more quickly.

Back-to-front

Try walking backward. Is this faster or slower than hopping?

Hop-a-long

Have a hopping race. First try your right leg, then your left. Is there a difference in the times?

On three legs

You may need to practice for a three-legged race! See if you can beat your own best time each time you try it.

Past times

People have measured the passage of time for thousands of years. First they used the movements of the sun to keep track of time. Have you ever noticed how a shadow from a tree moves during the day? You can tell the position of the sun in the sky by looking at the length of a shadow.

Be a shadow stick
On a sunny day, mark a spot on the ground and stand on it once every hour. Ask a friend to draw around your shadow each time. What do you notice about the shadow?

Sunshine and shadows

After a time, people used shadows to make a more accurate kind of clock, the sundial. Sundials are always outside, and they are often in gardens. Have you ever seen one? When is it impossible to tell the time with a sundial?

There are still many beautiful old sundials. They work just as well now as when they were new.

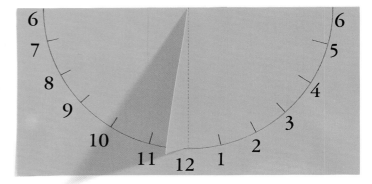

How sundials work
The shadow from the pointer falls on the sundial's face. The numbered markings show what time of day it is. As the Earth moves around the sun, the shadow moves across the sundial.

Candles and water

People also thought of other ways of marking the passage of time. They saw that burning candles of the same size took the same amount of time to melt away. They also realized that water would drip from one container into another at a steady rate. Candle and water clocks both work quite well as markers of time, but can you think of any problems you might have with them?

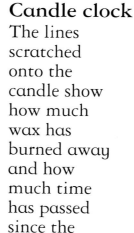

Candle clock
The lines scratched onto the candle show how much wax has burned away and how much time has passed since the candle was lit.

Water clock
The water drips through a small hole from one container into another. The bottom container fills with water as the hours pass.

28

Early clocks and watches

Mechanical clocks were first made about 700 years ago. But when the pendulum was invented 300 years later, clocks began to keep much better time. People also wanted to be able to know the time wherever they went, so they would carry pocket watches. Wristwatches became popular about 100 years ago. Today, most people wear watches all the time to keep track of their busy schedules!

Mechanical clock
Tightly coiled springs turn the gears. The gears make the hands move around at the right speed.

Pendulum clock
A hanging clock's pendulum swings back and forth. It takes exactly the same amount of time on each swing and moves the clock's hands around accurately.

Pocket watch
Pocket watches were used until quite recently. People carried them in their pockets, attached to a chain to keep them safe.

Wristwatch
People wear lots of different styles of watches. Some look like fancy jewelry and some look like colorful art.

Missing numbers

Many modern clocks and watches don't even have numbers on them! How can you tell which is the top?

- Can you tell the times on these clocks and watches?
- Move the hands of your fold-out clock to the same positions as these clocks and watches to check if you were right.

Playtime

Practice what you've learned about telling the time with these puzzles!

What goes with which?

- Which clock shows what time Bobby wakes up in the morning?
- Which clock shows when Joanne leaves for school?
- Which clock shows when Mark's mom gets home from work?
- Which clock shows when Anna eats her lunch?

Joanne   Bobby   Anna   Mark

How many ways to say. . .?

How many different ways can you say the times shown on these clocks and watches?

Fold-out fun

Try to answer these questions, using your fold-out clock to show the different times.

- What time do you usually wake up in the morning?
- What time does school start?
- What time is lunchtime?
- What time does school end?
- What time do you usually eat dinner?
- What's the earliest time you've ever woken up?

Roman numerals

Some clocks have numbers that you might not recognize. They are called **Roman numerals**. Have you ever seen a clock or watch with numbers like these on its face? Use the chart below to help you tell the time on these clocks.

I	II	III	*IIII	V	VI
1	2	3	4	5	6
VII	VIII	IX	X	XI	XII
7	8	9	10	11	12

* See note on page 32

Mix and match

Each of the times shown below matches one other time on the page.

When you find two times that match, cover the two boxes with coins or small pieces of paper.

Words about time

a.m. These letters stand for the Latin words, *ante meridian*, meaning "before noon." (page 24)

afternoon The part of the day between 12 o'clock noon and sunset is called afternoon. (page 7)

analog clock Analog clocks have an hour hand, a minute hand, and sometimes a second hand to show the time. (page 16)

calendar A calendar has a page for each month of the year. Each month's page shows every day of the month. (page 9)

clock Clocks have hands that move at a regular pace to help us keep track of time. (page 14)

clockface The part of a clock where you find the numbers and hands is called the clockface. (page 16)

clockwise The hands of a clock always move in the same direction, following the numbers from 1 to 12. This is called a clockwise direction. (page 16)

date A date is the day, month, and year when something happens. (page 9)

day There are 24 hours in a day. There are 365 days in a year. (page 6)

daytime From sunrise to sunset is daytime. It is light and you can usually see the sun. (page 6)

diary A diary shows all the days of a year. It has space for you to write down the things you do each day. (page 8)

digital clock Digital clocks and watches show the time with numbers instead of hands. (page 17)

evening The evening is the part of the day when the sun goes down and it gets darker, but it is not yet night. (page 6)

half past Half an hour is 30 minutes. Half past the hour is 30 minutes after the hour. (page 18)

hour There are 60 minutes in an hour and 24 hours in a day. (page 16)

long hand The long hand on a clockface is the minute hand. (page 16)

midnight Twelve o'clock in the middle of the night is called midnight. (page 24)

minute There are 60 seconds in a minute. There are 60 minutes in an hour. (page 20)

month There are about four weeks in a month. There are 12 months in a year: January, February, March, April, May, June, July, August, September, October, November, December. (page 9)

morning The part of the day between sunrise and noon is called morning. (page 6)

night From sunset to sunrise is night. It is dark and you can see the moon and stars. (page 6)

noon Twelve o'clock in the middle of the day is called noon. (page 24)

p.m. These letters stand for the Latin words, *post meridian*, meaning "after noon." (page 24)

quarter after A quarter of an hour is 15 minutes. Quarter after the hour is 15 minutes after the hour. (page 18)

quarter to A quarter of an hour is 15 minutes. Quarter to the hour is 15 minutes before the hour is up. (page 18)

Roman numerals Roman numerals are a set of numbers that were used a long time ago by the ancient Romans. We still use these numbers today. You may have seen them on clocks or watches. Roman numerals usually show 4 as IV, but on a clock, 4 is sometimes shown as IIII. (page 30)

season There are four seasons in a year: spring, summer, fall, winter. (page 10)

second There are 60 seconds in a minute. A part of a second is called a fraction of a second. (page 21)

short hand The short hand on a clockface is the hour hand. (page 16)

timer Although a timer looks like a clock, it doesn't tell us the time of day. Instead, it counts in minutes and seconds so that we can measure how long an activity or process takes. (page 27)

today Today is the present day – the day it is now. (page 8)

tomorrow Tomorrow is the day after today. It is in the future. (page 8)

watch A watch is a small clock that you can wear on your wrist. (page 14)

week There are seven days in a week: Sunday, Monday, Tuesday, Wednesday, Thursday, Friday, Saturday. (page 8)

weekend Together, Saturday and Sunday are called the weekend. (page 8)

year There are 12 months in a year. Ten years are called a decade. (page 9)

yesterday Yesterday is the day before today. It is in the past. (page 8)

Acknowledgements

Dorling Kindersley would like to thank the following for their help in producing this book:
Steve Shott; Dave King; Mark Richards; Steve Gorton; Siobhan Power; Anita Ruddell; Neil Morris for writing the initial synopsis; Snow and Rock for the use of ski equipment and clothing; Trevor Smith's Animal World; Neil Blaxill for the use of antique clocks and watches; HS Walsh and Sons Ltd for the use of clock parts.

Dorling Kindersley would also like to give special thanks to the following for appearing in this book:
Joanne Bacchus; Amy Bradsell; Hannah Capleton; Bobby Cooper; Benjamin Cowler; Billy Dunne; Sophie Gamba; Daniel Gregory; Rebecca Kern; William Lindsay; Catherine McAulay; Mark Natthan; Tebedge Ricketts; Cole Salewicz; Steve Shott; Beryl Simmonds; Dawn Sirett; Oliver Smith; Sonia Sullivan.

Picture Agency Credits
t=top; b=bottom; c=centre; l=left; r=right
Bruce Coleman Ltd: 28c; Image Bank: 15cl, 15c, 15bc;
Spectrum Colour Library: 15tl, 15tr; Zefa: 14tc, 14cl, 14br.

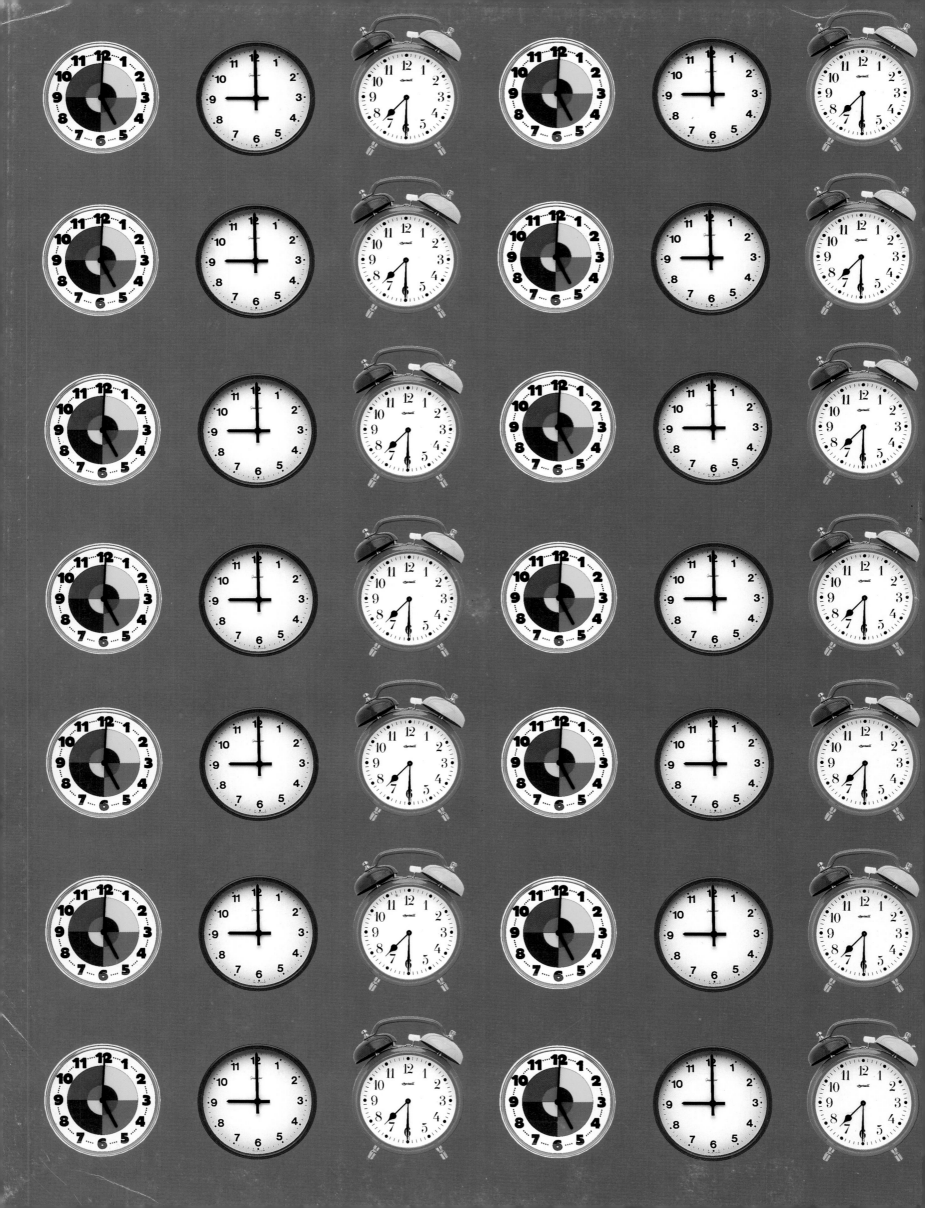